FASHION TRIBES CHINA

Edited by Kevin Tallon

FASHION TRIBES CHINA

Edited by Kevin Tallon

BATSFORD

First published in the United Kingdom in 2009 by
Batsford
10 Southcombe Street
London W14 0RA

An imprint of Anova Books Company Ltd

ISBN: 9781906388393

A CIP catalogue record for this book is available from the British Library.

16 15 14 13 12 10 09
10 9 8 7 6 5 4 3 2 1

Reproduction by Spectrum Colour, Ipswich
Printed in Malaysia

This book can be ordered direct from the publisher at the website www.anovabooks.com or try your local bookshop

Front Cover
'Jellymon x Reine et Roi' by Sam @ jellymon

Back Cover
'Dodo' by Paco HRD

Previous page

Beijing designer and
store owner for label
Lu 12.28.

CONTENTS

INTRODUCTION

History of Fashion Tribes

Over the last fifty years, street fashion has grown in importance as an influential socio-cultural popular movement, its roots traceable to before the Second World War in embryonic underground forms. The advent of mass media and the post-war American film industry pushed street fashion into the limelight and the popular conscience, illustrated by the seminal movies *The Wild One* (1953) and *Rebel Without a Cause* (1955). The power of James Dean's portrayal of the rebel with leather jacket, Greaser hair cut, white T-shirt and selvedge denim had such an impact that many teenagers tried to emulate the look. Although filmmakers were influenced by real rebels and bikers, they managed to promote the look and feel of youth rebellion to a much wider audience. The unique link between attitude, stance and specific attire was confirmed and established. Youths unconsciously understood that to stand out one should embrace a particular stylistic identity.

Once the wheels of youth rebellion were set in motion there was no stopping them – young Americans were craving more of what spoke directly to them. They soon found that music was another inherent part of a new-found youth identity and differentiation; Bill Haley's 'Rock Around the Clock' (1954) and Elvis Presley's own version of 'Hound Dog' (1956) sold over four million copies during that year alone. Fashion, music and instinctive tribal values became the three pillars of all youth movements to come. The United Kingdom, always heavily influenced by American cultural exports, was the natural first recipient for this new wave of youth culture – thus the UK spawned its own seminal 'street fashion tribes'. During the following decades all 'tribes' duplicated the same three tenets of sartorial style, musical genre and strict codes of conduct. Most importantly these youth factions were not manufactured but genuinely lived and born from peer influences and natural selection. Over the past half-century or more, Teds, Greasers, Mods, Punks, Skinheads, New Romantics, Goths, Casuals, Scallies, Chavs and Indie kids moulded, refined and affirmed the relevance of street tribes, each one of them with their unique scene, sounds and styles. The genuine origination of tribes became harder to ascertain over time; copycats, marketers and wheeler-dealers soon found out ways to cash in on the mass availability of 'off the peg' looks. Communication, mass media and the digital age have today extensively diluted what were once distinctive and genuine tribes into irrelevant flash-in-the pan sub-genre multiples. In our millennial age of attention-deficit kids and instant digital gratification, genuine affiliation to street tribes is hard to come by, but the endless outflow of changing looks and genres has enabled the birth of cool hunting.

Top: Teddy Boy by Paolo Mointegnacco
Below: Mod & Rocker by David Zellaby

Cool Hunting

While a general awareness of major street tribes was common knowledge in previous decades, the faster-changing pace of street culture and its tendency to split into sub-genres (think of dance music as a good brainteaser) have made it trickier for the general public to grasp them today. Coupled with this was the relentless drive for self-promotion where being unique was a must in the light of style copycats encroaching the 'genuines' turf. Fashion street tribes came in all shades and distinguishing an Acid-jazzer from a Northern Souler was becoming difficult. In the early nineties, marketers started to panic – they could not grasp those minute differentiations so decided to fight back: they sent out teams of young and trendy 'Cool Hunters' who understood the 'hunted' tribes. The hunters were to spend time on the streets, in the clubs, observing what tribes were buying, wearing, consuming, and listening to. They could sell their findings back to their corporate clients with the latest street words, looks and sounds. Not long after this development, the way in which 'the cool' were captured began to change. Driven by the growing mass availability of digital media platforms and media-recording devices, street fashion amateurs started to experiment and photograph cool people for little or no cost. This radically changed what was previously a strictly professionals-only business, with photo-journalists using expensive and complicated analogue gear on commission for style magazines. A new breed of amateur Cool Hunters was working in the undergrowth.

Digital Revolution

The digital revolution carried on at a frantic pace, increasing in power and speed. The mass availability of faster broadband-based internet during the early to mid-'noughties' heralded a new era. Uploading a few pictures now took moments. As users discovered the joys of fast, cheap and constant surfing, they developed new ways of interacting with the web. Blogs began appearing in the mid-nineties and luminaries such as Matt Drudge and his Drudge Report were the first to break the news about Monica Lewinsky's affairs in 1998. This highlighted the fact that armed with a computer, broadband and a good insider's knowledge, anyone could challenge the media moguls. This democratisation of information and media platforms helped young people gain the confidence to start expressing themselves online through communities, diaries, blogs and forums. Soon blogging became easy with ready-made, technogeek-free services such as Blogger, bought by Google in 2003, and made free with, crucially, the addition of photo-sharing utility Picasa the following year. Cool hunting changed overnight, with every other kid able to shoot and post his or her day's hunting in no time and at no cost. Once the dust settled, seminal blogs such as Face Hunter, Style Scout, Style Slicker, Diane Pernet's A Shaded View on Fashion and Style Bubble, amongst others, raised the standard, which showed what was needed to stand out in the crowded blogsphere. As we enter the 'teen' decade, new foms of cool-hunting sites, such as Lookbook.nu, are appearing where the 'cool ones' are not merely hunted but actually posting their own looks with like-minded people.

Crowd at Central Saint Martins Fashion Press Show 2008 by Kevin Tallon

Birth of China Cool

Until the mid-seventies, China was still a closed and introspective society concerned with strict self-imposed policies instigated by Mao ZeDong's Cultural Revolution. Deng Xiaoping – the first leader to visit the USA in 1979 – understood that in order to evolve and modernize, China needed to reach out. Xiaoping focused the reforms on the economic sector and initiated an 'Open Door Policy' in specifically designated areas (Special Economic Zones, or SEZ) strategically located close to overseas Chinese communities such as Hong Kong, Taiwan and Macau. These reforms encouraged foreign investments, tax breaks and the building of infrastructures, such as factories and transport links. The policy had a dramatic impact on towns inside the SEZ, such as Shenzhen. Located on the mainland close to Hong Kong, this small town of 20,000 in 1980 grew at breakneck pace to become a manufacturing powerhouse of over 5 million inhabitants in less than 25 years.

The Open Door policy was a huge success for China both economically and politically; it also enabled the birth of a consumer culture. While consuming does not necessarily lead to freedom of speech it provides a kind of freedom of expression in the most innocuous of ways: style and status. Consuming became good, consuming became communist! These big economical reforms have had a major socio-cultural impact on the Chinese population living in big cities. The freedoms attached to consumerism have empowered young people with a sense of individuality and self esteem rarely experienced by previous Chinese generations. These new forms of expression have been embraced mainly by a younger Chinese generation in tune with the global digital revolution and its fast delivery of media content, enabling China to dramatically catch up with the rest of the world when it comes to maturity of style and self-confidence.

Above: 'Guangzhou Girls', 1979, David Gedawel
Above: 'Young soldiers enjoying time off',
Beijing, Alexander Dluzak.

Fashion Tribes China

China finds itself in a confident place. The world has witnessed how far it has come from the Middle Kingdom in the past 30 years. The balance of influence is slowly shifting and with the new millennium maturing, China should be set to become the new super-power. Even if the West wants China to tackle key political and socio-cultural issues, its size alone makes it a major international and influential player whether it does or not. Over the past two years, on my countless trips to Beijing, I have witnessed first hand the fast pace of change taking place in China's capital. From a country selling cheap cigarettes, food, and a plethora of fake goods from DVD to Chanel bags, China is now an outstanding shopping destination where flagship stores are cropping up at an amazing pace. China's consumer industry need take no lessons from Western shopping malls.

The changing social and economic climate in China has had a direct impact on the nation's youth. Having emerged from a twentieth century of creative repression and a long history of valued collectivism, the present generation of young Chinese people are at the forefront of a momentous cultural shift. Approaches to style and fashion have changed dramatically. The focus on freedom of expression – influenced in part by Japan and the West – has replaced the conformity and neutrality, which had lingered since the Cultural Revolution. Consequently, numerous groups or 'tribes' have emerged, and while the majority of those with

Above right: 'Untitled' By Jason
Above left: 'Yuzuki' by Paco HRD

disposable incomes are content to buy into designer labels, many of the younger generation are exploring the possibilities of vintage, alternative and independent aesthetics. The new-found freedom has not, however, quashed the innate pride in Chinese culture and heritage; symbols, icons and references to the country's own vast history and accomplishments retain a vital place in contemporary Chinese fashion. But while these deep-rooted values are retained and shared amongst young Chinese people, the fashion tribes have evolved in distinctly different directions, ranging from alternative, iconic dressing to hip hop and sportswear. In China, trendy fashion-conscious people are known as *Chao Ren* (literally meaning wave people, as in people surfing waves of style, constantly looking for the new wave).

For this book, I have spent countless hours with my team editing pictures to provide a visual journey, establishing a seamless spectrum of style within each tribe. Casual Sports, for example, begins with fashionable people wearing loose-cut denim and canvas shoes with a touch of sportiness usually translated by a polo shirt or a vintage tracksuit top. The tribe then makes the transition to a more mainstream, casual look to finish with full-on sports fans. I hope this book will give readers a good insight into China's key fashion tribes and prove beyond doubt that China's youth are on trend and will soon influence the rest of the world with their own style, culture and vision of what being 'cool' is all about.

Kevin Tallon

01. ALTERNATIVES

A lifestyle as much as a fashion statement, the Alternative scene has an underlying rejection of Chinese convention at its core. In a country undergoing massive socio-economic changes, the Alternative tribe consists of young, like-minded individuals who are seizing the 'freedom' that China's new governance allows and putting their enthusiasm to alternative and non-mainstream creative use.

Street-centered social gatherings, often focused around group activities such as skateboarding or street art, are central to this scene. Within these regular congregations, ideas are shared and the world of fashion, music and art are explored and teased with a punk attitude that was, until recently, unheard of in China. But while discovering the possibilities within the country's newly adopted open-mindedness, the boundaries are known and respected.

An interest in alternative culture is rapidly catching on amongst China's youth, but the country is still, comparatively, in its fashion infancy and relatively few are brave enough to overstep the perimeters of conventional national dress for fear of 'social alienation[1]'. But a sense of creative experimentation in the fashion scene is growing. Even tattoos, formerly frowned upon because of its association with criminal markings and enforced conformism during the Cultural Revolution, are now 'becoming an increasingly popular way to express identity[2].' While foreign brands associated with independent culture such as Vans and Converse are an inherent part of the Alternative movement in China, many young Chinese entrepreneurs are starting up their own 'underground' boutiques and labels, particularly in areas such as Beijing's Gulou district. There is a strong willingness to support and celebrate local, independent Chinese enterprises within this community, with home-grown labels such as the ubiquitous Monkey Style (see page 28) making a cult impact. At the same time, China's alternative music and art scene is expanding, with independent record labels, galleries in the famous 798 district, music festivals like Notch, and underground punk-rock bands such as the rebellious Subs – 'riotous explosions of pure energy rare to the Middle Kingdom[3]' – revealing the mine of talent that this adrenaline-fuelled generation has to offer. In fact, with more social and political issues in their recent history to react against, Chinese punk bands seem to have more credibility than many of their European counterparts. 'Holding to the spirit of independent music, many Chinese bands are producing truly original music and often you can hear traditional Chinese musical influences[4].'

The Alternative tribe is inclusive and open-minded, with a strong belief in the country's progress that underpins the optimism and hope for the future that this generation is displaying. The young people who constitute this tribe are prepared to challenge themselves to create their own success and live by their own rules; their 'no fear' outlook is one that is quickly evolving and expanding. Aware of the creative potential inherent in the changing political outlook of China, the limits of their ambition continue to be pushed.

Above: SOSO, ViVID and her friends.

Within this tribe are several niche groups with different sources of fashion influence. The indie look, still seen in the Western alternative scene, forms one of the key sub-tribes, epitomised by skinny jeans and slim, often pointed, shoes adorning frail frames, with hair kept long and deliberately unkempt. Branching out from this look are the edgier individuals, baring prominent tattoos to indelibly mark their commitment to the alternative lifestyle. Accessories are a popular means of expressing individuality amongst both sexes, with key chains, lip and ear piercings and wrist beads featuring strongly. The skateboarding dress code is also a predominant one. While it remains a mostly male pastime, women constitute an important part of this group, often dressing androgynously to fit with the masculine Alternative-Action look. Trucker caps, skate shoes, low-slung jeans, graphic T-shirts and baggy shorts can be seen on both men and women. Also central to many in the Alternatives tribe is the growing music scene, and clothes are worn to display this interest. Headphones are worn over beanies, with band T-shirts and clubbing clothes that match their semi-nocturnal lifestyle. Finally, there is a vibrant Alternatives art scene with countless budding performance and fine artists, photographers, writers, video directors and grafitti artists. They all experiment with their wardrobes, nurturing and expressing new forms of genuine sartorial creativity.

Left: Oz, Graphic Designer

Right: Plenty of Rockers can be seen around the districts of Beijing, taking their cue from either Rockabilly or Brit Rockers with D-cut hair or shaggy fringes separating the two.

Below: Hats, particularly Fedoras, are making a comeback. Capturing the current fascination with hats on boys, these two photographers have a certain louche aura about them.

Right: Young film student.

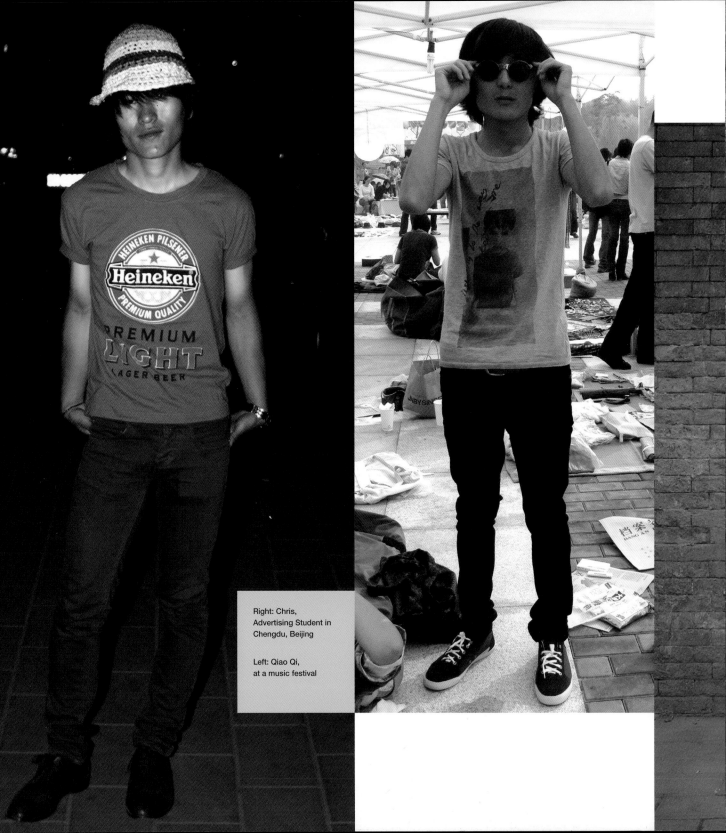

Right: Chris,
Advertising Student in
Chengdu, Beijing

Left: Qiao Qi,
at a music festival

Left: Bo Xuan,
Bassist from Hedgehog

Right: Converse trainers, an international symbol of free thinking and youth, teamed with skinny jeans made a comeback. This Beijinger completes the look with narrow, colour-matching braces.

Left: Gia W
Lead Singer of Hang
On The Box

Right: Drifter in
Nanluoguxiang

Left: 'D' (Lead singer of the band, D and the Hutong Cats). Nam bank

Right: Slim Akira General Manager of D-22.

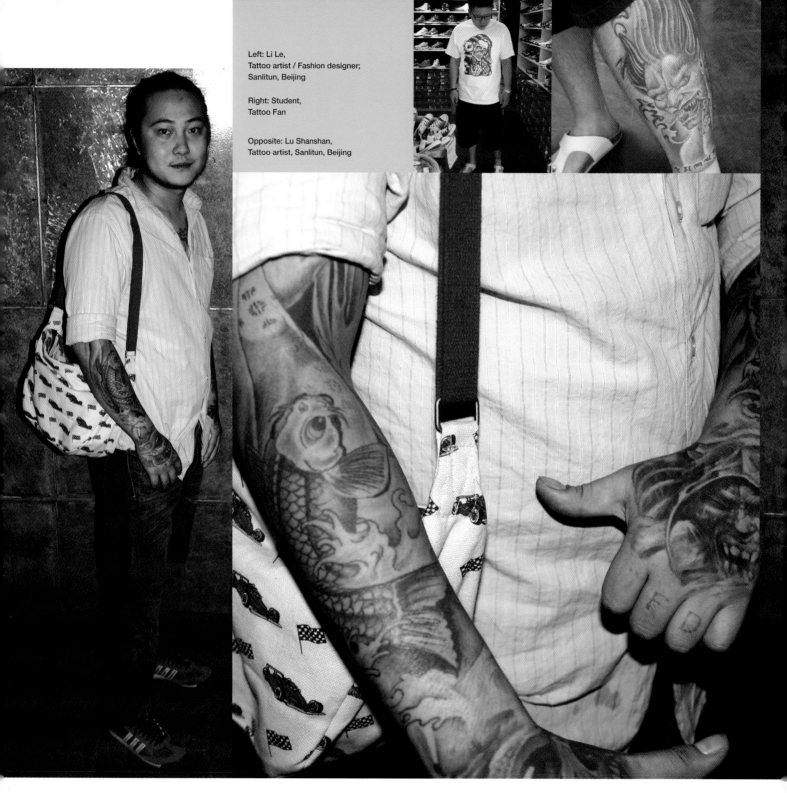

Left: Li Le,
Tattoo artist / Fashion designer;
Sanlitun, Beijing

Right: Student,
Tattoo Fan

Opposite: Lu Shanshan,
Tattoo artist, Sanlitun, Beijing

Zhao Xiaoqing;
Medical Student and
Shop Owner.
Wangfujing, Beijing

Left and above: Skater showing off his tattos, Gulo district, Beijing

Right: Partygoer at the Mix Club of Worker's Stadium, Beijing

Opposite: Clubber at Mao Club, Beijing

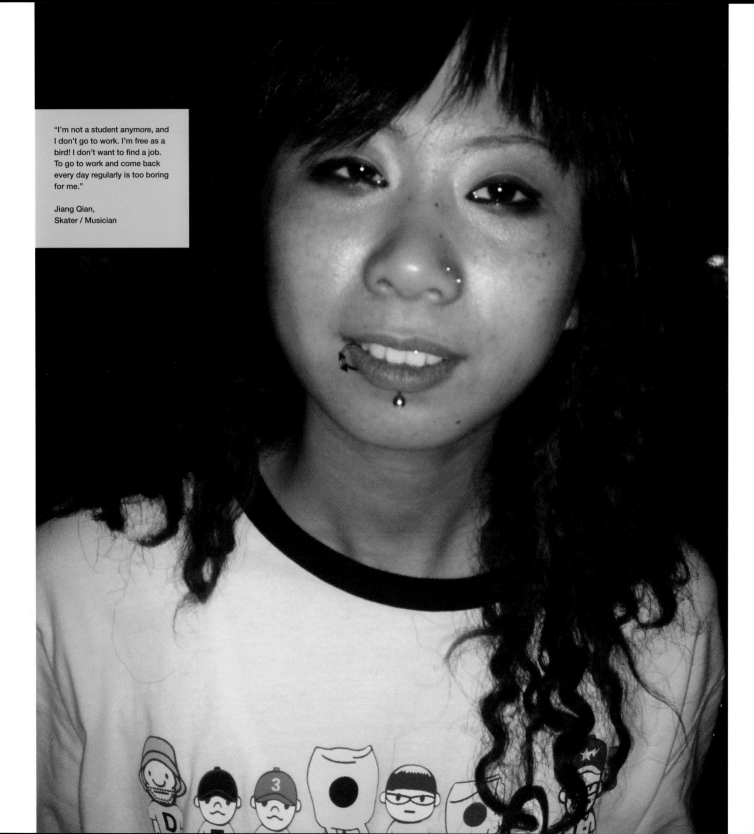

"I'm not a student anymore, and I don't go to work. I'm free as a bird! I don't want to find a job. To go to work and come back every day regularly is too boring for me."

Jiang Qian,
Skater / Musician

Partygoers at the Mix Club
of Worker's Stadium, Beijing

Kerry Fang, 24
Bartender, Sanlitun

Clockwise from top left: 3-D
designer in Multimedia Design
Agency
Jianwai SoHo, Beijing

China's top street label collector,
East Gulo Street, Beijing

Student / Skater
Xidan

Street Fashion shop owner in
Monkey Style Store, Beijing

BURN
YOUR
LIFE

Opposite and left: Gulo,
shop stalkers

Right: Lucky Street near
Chaoyang Park, Beijing

Du Peng,
DJ, Sanlitun, Beijing

Du Peng,
DJ, Sanlitun, Beijing

Right: 'Guanyin'
Member of Beijing graffiti
crew

Above left: Graffiti artist

Left: Student waiting
outside the subway, Xidan
Beijing

Opposite: 'Bite Coco'

Above: 'Hidden Mood'

Right: 'No Face'

Above: 'Float'

Left and opposite: Untitled

O2. IC⊙NICS

Beyond the era of social oppression and enforced conformity that dominated the country in previous years, a small minority of China's youth have begun to explore the potential of true individualism.

Emerging from the creative stagnation of the twentieth century with the fresh notion that anything is possible, self expression and subversion in the sphere of fashion is being adopted by this group of Iconics – perhaps timidly at first, but with inspirational encouragement from Japan and the West, a unique approach is taking shape within China.

As with some other tribes, an important motivator for members of the Iconic tribe is rebellion albeit on a purely sartorial level. Before the 2008 Beijing Olympics, local officials distributed over four million copies of an etiquette book that included rules of appropriate dress. The book states, 'No matter what, never wear too many colours... especially during formal occasions[5]'. In the pursuit of individuality, Iconics rebel against archaic fashion rules and resist uniformity. Patronage of home-grown designers is also important. Estune, a quirky boutique in Shanghai, stocks independent Chinese labels that break the mould and make designs for those with the same intentions. 'In China, what we sell most of here are the things with writing on or with ornaments sewn on. Chinese consumers like things that jangle[6].'

While prominent brands such as Prada and Chanel retain a grip on the majority of China's nouveau riche, the Iconic tribe nurtures an interest in more avant-garde designers, such as the less conspicuous labels of Comme des Garçons and Yohji Yamamoto. The potential of vintage and, in particular, eighties retro are also starting to be explored by the more cutting edge – indie magazine *Kungfu*, established in China in August 2008, recognises vintage and retro fashion as an up-and-coming trend amongst China's youth. 'Simple, innocent and silly' and with 'elements that everyone of the generation can recognise and relate to' are key factors outlined in the magazine that define the approach taken towards retro clothing. Mixing up big labels with cheap vintage (such as the iconic People Liberation Army winter coat) and lesser-known designer garments is a rapidly growing trend, and accessories are added to heighten the individuality of the look and dismantle traditional outfits. Chunky Doc Marten's boots are contrasted with feminine dresses and coloured tights, while multicoloured shoelaces transform plain pumps.

Japan has always been at the forefront of eccentric street fashion, and many amongst the Chinese Iconic tribe are emulating the Japanese Goth, Ganguro and Lolita styles. But China isn't far behind in forming its own, localized aesthetic. While Iconic dress trends in Japan typically reflect the country's popular culture, there is a

'Pop Boy'

trend in China that leans towards its own social history with military hats, high collars and boots that accompany austere black bicycles, reminiscent of the Cultural Revolution era. In keeping with this trend, China-based T-shirt company Plastered depict relics of the past nostalgically in its designs, with references to ancient Chinese objects and traditions, highlighted with the distinctive colours of the Chinese flag. Similarly, *Book of Warriors* by Shumeng Ye refers to the iconic 'Warrior' trainers of the seventies that are now worn mainly by peasants and the elderly. Their transition from status symbol to the purely functional is recorded with sensitive insight, emphasising the fact that young Chinese people are keen to preserve their own history while developing new trends; a process of regurgitating the past, which is continuously occurring in Western fashion. While the country's long-established collective mentality remains, individuality is also being embraced, resulting in a unique kind of individualism where the 'rebellion' is devoid of the cynicism and irony present amongst Western youth, with a nod towards China's ancient heritage.

The sub-tribes within the Iconics take quite different approaches to dress. There are those who are influenced by Tokyo- and London-centric catwalk fashion, currently with 'tramp' boots, PVC leggings and eighties hats, though the look is never without their own Chinese touch and is often accompanied by the compulsory little Chanel handbag. In quite a distinctive turn in direction, another group allude to the classic British punk era with ripped jeans, battered Doc Marten's, flame-red hair and copious amounts of pins and badges. Then there are the art-house, conceptual dressers, again taking inspiration from London and New York with well-considered components of vintage. The forties coats are paired with retro sunglasses and one-off items from local, independent boutiques.

The 'austere' dressers, mentioned earlier, have taken to retro clothing. They favour black and grey. A modern androgynous feel is created from the conservative shirts and tailored jackets worn by both the men and women in this group. Conversely, the Japanese kitsch, Manga cartoon image is also being reproduced, with candy-coloured, knee-high stripy socks, loud colours and backcombed hair. And then there are the extroverts; the exhibitionists redolent of London club kids that dress to cause a stir, with supernatural hair colours, pierced tongues and comedic, outsized glasses that succeed in drawing the attention that is desired. Chinese Iconics are a tribe to watch out for in the near future. With potentially limitless forms of expression and genuine creativity, they are bound to carry on challenging the blurry dress code boundaries set by the authorities.

Jellymon x Reine et Roi

Left: Xiang, Music
Producer
Dong Shan

Right: Diesa,
Music Producer
Dong Shan

Left: Pink, Freelancer
Bao Yuan Road

Right: Ying, Music
Producer
Dong Shan

Above: Alison, Singer
Dong Shan

Right: Momoko,
Music Player
Dong Shan

藝術書店
Arts Book Store

合作
服务

转让尚雯婕 3.1
演唱会票 2 张
原价 333 元/张
书店内面议

无需排队!
快速报名

打报名表

快照

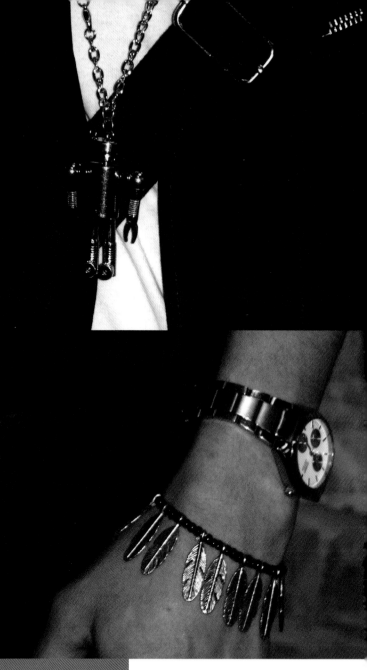

Hillben Ho, Fashion Editor
798 District, Beijing

Above: Hitomi
Oyama,
Translator/ freelance
journalist, writing for
both Chinese
and Japanese
publications.

Right: Gao Jian,
Modern Dancer

Left: Allen,
Freelance journalist

Right: Sabrina,
Account Executive
at Ogilvy PR

Opposite right: Liang Qiao,
Stylist, 798 District, Beijing

Opposite left: Zhang Zheming,
Photographer, 798 District, Beijing

Below: Cult Warrior (Hui Li)
trainers

Left: Halla,
Shopping and Travel Editor of
The *Beijinger* magazine

Above: Laura,
Freelance Journalist for a range
of mainland publications,
including *Modern Weekly* and
Vogue

Opposite: Liu Lu, (both
pictures)
Beijing designer and store
owner for label 'Lu 12.28'
with ready-to-wear and
haute couture lines.

Jiang Jungao, Fashion Designer

Wang Jieyu, Fashion
Student, Raffles Design
Institute

Ming, Make-up Artist,
Chang Gang East Road

Wu Ying and Zhang Guangyuan,
Civil engineering students

Opposite right: Lin Lin,
Chinese Stylist
Roppongi Hills, Tokyo

Xie Xin, Stylist
798 District, Beijing

Left: Richard Lu,
Founder and CEO of
Classical Public
Relations Co., Ltd

Above: Li Benben,
Student

Opposite: Wang Hui,
Unemployed, Beijing

Above: 'Me at 30'

Left: Jacky, Student

Opposite: Jacky with friends, Zhonghua Square

03. HIP HOP

The global phenomenon of hip hop culture has made its mark in China. In the cultural capital of Shanghai, 37 per cent of 15- to 25-year-olds prefer rap and hip hop to any other musical genre[7]. But to some, hip hop represents an entire lifestyle, conveying a message that speaks to the Chinese youth of anti-establishment whilst offering an antidote to the saccharine pop stars that infiltrate the mainstream media.

The clothing only constitutes a part, the surface manifestation, of the genre's entity. True dedication to hip hop as a way of life involves listening to associated music, appreciated for its frankness and straightforward language 'to express true feeling and genuine reality[8]'. And, for many, hip hop break-dancing is also central to everyday life. With names such as 'D Day Crew' and 'Crazy Park', local teams congregate daily to practice and perform in the street. Often very team work-orientated, this pastime has become extremely popular amongst young Chinese people who, on the whole, value fitness and sociable activities as priorities in life.

Many girls partake in hip hop dancing, but others prefer simply to dress in this style, copying the A-shape look of the boys with close-fitted vests and loose trousers. Indeed, not everyone who appreciates the hip hop aesthetic is devoted to the lifestyle it entails. Some regard it as a commercial trend that can be used casually, a 'bling dynasty' fashion movement that allows them to dress in huge hoodies and gold chains. Sharing some characteristics with the sports tribe, the hip hop style is often defined by baggy-fitting garments, denim, oversized T-shirts and baseball caps, all enhanced with large, ostentatious watches and jewellery.

Although inspired largely by American hip hop culture, the Chinese approach is very different, as it is fundamentally neither cynical nor accusatory. Many Chinese hip-hoppers have a positive focus on study and progression rather than rebellion, and are modest, polite and supportive of one another. However, MCs and rappers are constantly pushing the limits of what constitutes acceptable lyrical content in a sort of cat and mouse game with the authorities. As is the case with many other countries, the birth of Chinese hip hop has developed from an emulation of American icons rather than first-hand experience of its origins in the 'ghetto' environment and has hence taken a unique direction within the genre. Hip hop predecessors in neighbouring Korea have also been heavily influential on the development of the genre in China, particularly within the realm of dance and street performance.

In a similar vein to the French and German scenes, Chinese hip hop communicates to its audience by localising its message and making it personally – and nationally – relevant. 'Hip hop comes from the US, but we are using Chinese content. We like this kind of music, but we are also passionate about Chinese culture and Beijing culture. We are combining them in our music[9],' says 17-year-old student, Sun Xiao. Dan Stephenson, a promoter and DJ, commends Chinese hip hop's ability to retain its own cultural identity. 'Beijing is international; it's a city of the world. The [artists] out there are localising it. Wholesale emulation is at an end. It's international. The young absorb a lot of the cultural influences, communication, dress and give it a Chinese tweak[10].'

2008 UK B-Boy
championships, North
East China eliminations.
Dalian city.

Western basketball is readily embraced within the hip hop realm. With many young Chinese people idolising basketball heroes like Tracy McGrady and LeBron James, their love of hip hop is only secondary to their love of the sport. MC and executive chief editor of *Hip-Hop* magazine Gao Mengbo started enjoying rap music because of his basketball hero Allen Iverson[11]. The dress code for this group is often similar to that of the Sports tribe (see page 126), with long basketball vests and Pro Signature Basketball footwear. The physical activity involved for the dancers requires this kind of dress – loose-fitting clothes and rolled-up trousers are all but essential. The street look is more toned down but still label-conscious, with an emphasis on accessories and 'big and blinging[12]' jewellery. Chunky chains, watches, baseball caps and wristbands are worn with rucksacks for a heavy, masculine look, with many sporting large, sprawling tattoos with traditional Chinese references. Rolled-up jeans, graphic T-shirts and detailing on accessories have a more nocturnal feel, worn from the streets to the underground gigs and clubs where this subculture gathers. The Chinese hip hop movement is starting to gather recognition, exemplified by Adidas Beijing flagship store's recent photographic exhibition entitled 'Be all I can be' where portraits of the tribe's key movers and shakers adorn the gallery walls.

2008 UK B-Boy
championships, North
East China eliminations.
Dalian city.

Clockwise from top:
Girl from the 2008 UK B-Boy
Championships, Dalian city; Boy
from 2008 B-Boy
Championships; STP Breakdance
crew; Graffiti Crew, Beijing

Weize,
Owner of hip hop store in
Gulou Dong Da Jie.

High school student,
University of International
Business and Economics

Sun Xu,
member of Ablaze Crew

Sun Xiao,
Finance student

Feng Wenjian,
798 district, Beijing

Zhang Hui, Student
Hip hop fan

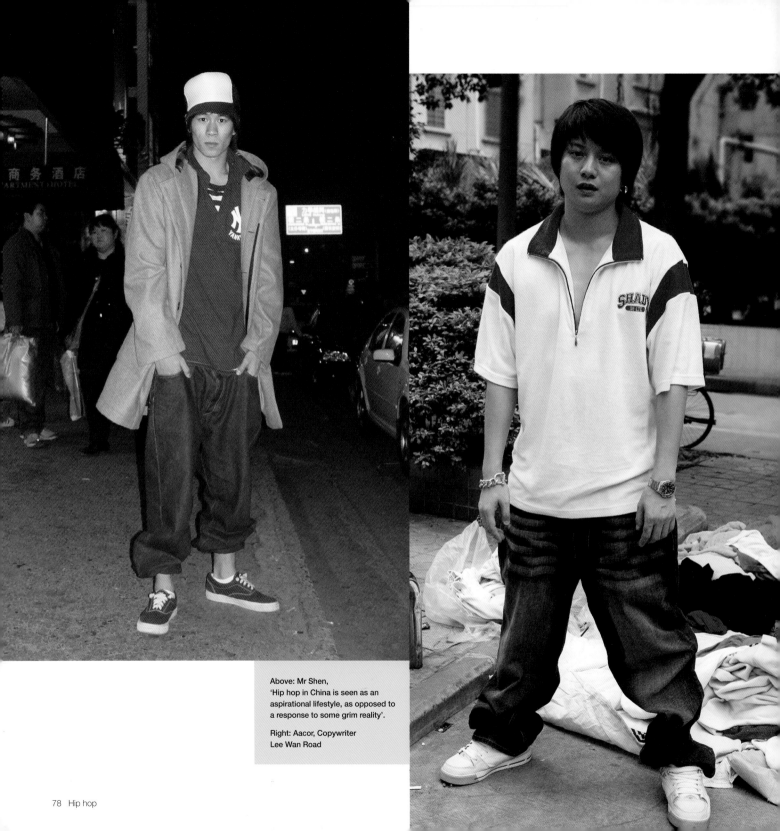

Above: Mr Shen,
'Hip hop in China is seen as an aspirational lifestyle, as opposed to a response to some grim reality'.

Right: Aacor, Copywriter
Lee Wan Road

Above: Aspiring DJ,
Nanluoguxiang

Far left: Orange, Dancer,
Bao Yuan Road

Below left: Cheerleader,
Dong Dang Sports Stadium

Katsura Humi from Japan,
office worker

Sam Lee,
Actor and Designer

Vernie Young,
Commercial Director

Left: Wize, Freelancer,
Lee Wan Road

Above: MC; Sanlitun,
Beijing

Qun Dian Luo Bu, Beijing

Opposite: MC, Sanlitun, Beijing

Above and right: MC4, Rapper,
Gulou

Above: Girls at a hip hop party, Chengdu

Left: Hip Hop fans,
Yu Gong Yi Shan Club, Beijing

Above: Prosa Crew, Guangzhou
Their song 'My Generation' is
banned in China

Left: MC 'Sbazzo' from a rap
crew called 'Yin Tsang'

O4.FASHIONISTAS

Continually updating their wardrobes with the latest 'must-haves', Fashionistas strive to keep up with the endless cycle of current trends. For some, the priority is the designer label, but high-street chain products are fast becoming a popular alternative for those craving a quick and inexpensive fashion fix.

After the initial surge of luxury brands such as Gucci and Prada into China, the recent arrival and expansion of 'fast fashion' chains means cheap and chic clothing has become more accessible. Since the country's widening 'Open Door' policy, international brands have rushed towards its burgeoning fashion market, with new stores opening throughout China's key cities. Those with newly acquired disposable incomes have begun to follow the indulgent habit of the Western consumer – buying into transient clothing trends that will be replaced after a season or two. Indicatively, when asked what her biggest expenditure was, 20-year-old Dou Dou from Beijing didn't hesitate to reveal her vice: 'Shopping. Mostly buying clothes for me. I'll spend 4,000 Yuan when I have made 2,000[13].'

With China's growing economic confidence, it is not surprising that retailers are pouncing on this new generation of consumers with credit cards, disposable incomes and a penchant for flashing cash. Equipped with a spending power of more than $3.3 trillion (2007), China's nouveau riche youth proudly don their Louis Vuitton bags, Dior belts and Louboutin heels, affirming their social status through brand name-buying; 'a recent study [2006–07] of middle-class families in Asia by the market research firm CLSA found that 85% of middle-income families interviewed in China owned at least one credit or debit card. More than half of this group used their cards to go shopping[14].' Dominated by young women aged 20 to 35, the 'nouveau riche' are largely still living with their parents. Without the expenditure of rent and bills, they have significantly higher disposable incomes and can easily afford to pay extra for a lusted-after designer bag.

A cultural emphasis on collectivism in China can explain the desire to fit in and dress similarly, while the roots of the Fashionista tribe could also be traced to Confucianism and the importance of 'family face[15]'. As a successful public 'face' is growing throughout the country with its 10,000 Chinese entrepreneurs possessing $10 million or more[16], luxury brands can be regarded as a way to flaunt a family's wealth. Taking advantage of China's increasingly lavish spending, fashion houses have begun to host shows in major Chinese centres – Karl Lagerfeld, for example, used The Great Wall of China as an extravagant runway for a 2007 Fendi collection.

As the popularity of high-end products continues to soar, mere imitations are a definite fashion faux pas amongst the nouveau riche. While the World Trade Organisation continues its combat against designer copycats, sites like Fakehunter aid consumers in spotting counterfeit goods as the Chinese become more and more discerning with their tastes. Opting for 'authentic' luxury, even toiletries are not exempt from a critical eye; 25-year-old Wu Sha says she always buys her shampoo from Tesco, 'because I know it is not a fake[17].'

Students Qiqi and friend, Zhonghua Square.

This consumer trend is combined with the growth of online social networking, with many young people opting for local platforms, such as QQ, which leads the market with a reported 300 million active accounts[18]. Xiaonei (a Facebook copycat) has recently raised over $430 million, thus challenging plans for the American giant to muscle its way into the Chinese social networking market.

Global blogs and online magazines enable ideas and trends to be shared quickly and easily, meaning Chinese Fashionistas are exposed to and influenced by the fashion and lifestyles of their European, Japanese and American equivalents. 'Social networking services have become a pivotal part of the online life of Chinese youth[19].' Online Chinese fashion blogs that document trends from abroad, such as Street Chic, suggest that Western fashion is still followed, but Chinese Fashionistas have quickly evolved from a tentative, copycat start to a self-assured and directional style.

Shanghai Viva, a cool-hunting website that focuses on the street apparel of the country's fashion capital, is testament to this. For the younger 'fast' Fashionistas that are looking to high-street chains for influence, there is a positive energy in their attire that reflects the sense of confidence in their country's future. For these followers of the less expensive fashion trail, European brands such as Zara and H&M have already set up shop in Shanghai and Beijing, with American brands such as Banana Republic, American Apparel and Urban Outfitters following suit. For women, the look tends to be understated and girlish, often finished off with tiny handbags – preferably Chanel. Denim micro-shorts, mini skirts and tight-fitting T-shirts also make a frequent appearance, and hair is kept long and worn down. Slim-fitting jeans, sunglasses, graphic prints, slogans on T-shirts and sleek haircuts are important features for both sexes. Importantly, all the clothes worn by this tribe appear brand new and well looked-after – scruffiness, for men or women, would be considered a glaring mistake. Other Fashionistas have a more 'student' look with clothes that are, although still clean-cut, slightly more edgy and playful. The girls seem tomboyish, with long-tongued Converse canvas shoes, polo shirts and knee length shorts, and the look is similar for the men but usually completed with a leather belt and a large, square shoulder bag. Retro is embraced by some, but items are chosen carefully to conform with current trends. Patterns abound on feminine dresses, worn with tights and high heels, and finished with a long-strapped handbag. For the more mature, professional Fashionista, luxury suits and formal wear is broken down and made youthful with accessories and flashes of luminous colour.

For this generation of Chinese people, luxury symbolises a shared interest, an ideological pathway to the modern world. Optimism and light-heartedness are therefore central to this fashion movement.

Yuka, dancer, Dong Shan

Above: Shopper at
Wangfujing, Beijing

Right: Su Su, student

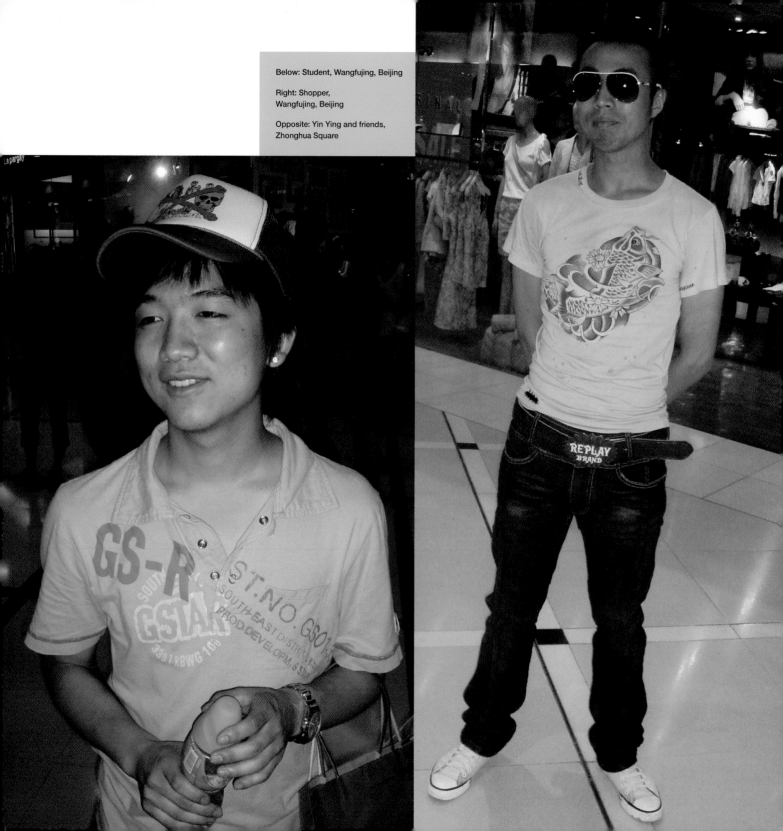

Below: Student, Wangfujing, Beijing

Right: Shopper,
Wangfujing, Beijing

Opposite: Yin Ying and friends,
Zhonghua Square

Above: University girl, Wang Fujing

Right: Kiki and Cici, fashion buyers, Zhonghua Square

Graphic Design student,
Wangfujing

Students, Wangfujing, Beijing

Student,
Beijing Institute of Clothing
Technology

Left and above: Li, student
Fashion Store in Shenyang

Opposite left: Yang Ming, Student

Opposite right: Clubber at Mix club of Worker's
Stadium

Pae Lewng, Model

'Vintage and second-hand clothing are slowly infiltrating the fashion-forward scene in Mainland China'.

Wang Ting,
Fashion student

Above: Partygoers at Mix club of Worker's Stadium

Opposite left: Jian Wai, singer, SoHo

Opposite right: Kiki,
Lead singer of Milk and Coffee on her way to rehearsal.

Opposite: Veronica Wang, Art Officer,
Tian He

Right: Interest, Student,
Xi Men Kou

Above: Young shoppers,
SoHo area, Beijing

Opposite: Lynn, Student,
University Town

Above: Art School student,
798 Art District, Beijing

Far left: Art School student,
798 Art District, Beijing

Left: Student, 798 Art
District, Beijing

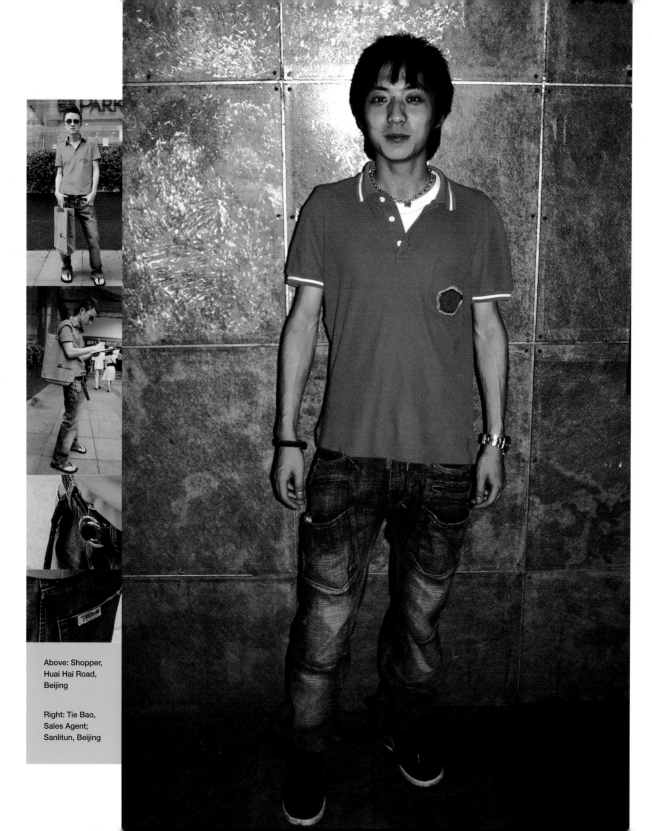

Above: Shopper,
Huai Hai Road,
Beijing

Right: Tie Bao,
Sales Agent;
Sanlitun, Beijing

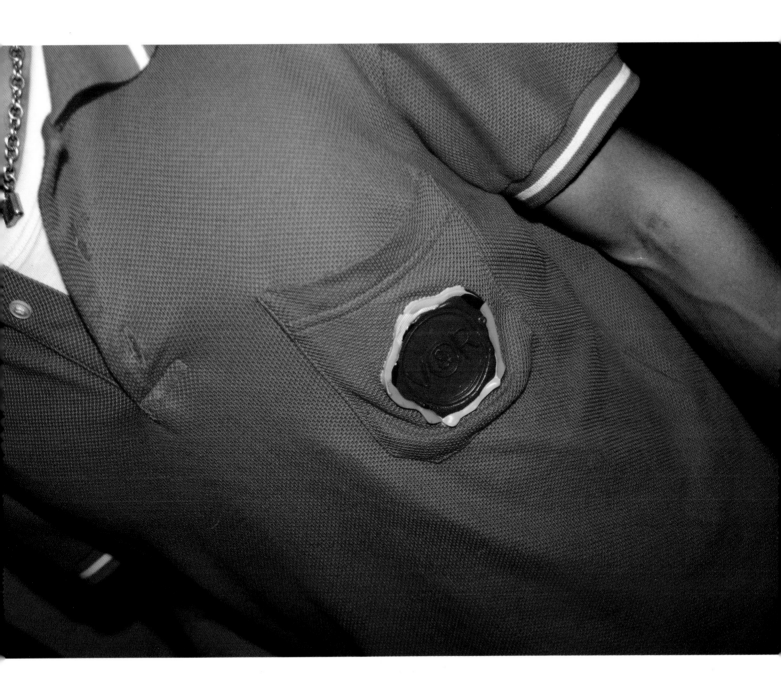

Ma Ke,
Photographer; Sanlitun,
Beijing

Shopper (loves mixing
luxury brands with
casual wear),
Xi Dan, Beijing

Left: Student, Raffles
Design Institute

Right: Zhao Bing,
Fashion Designer

Left: Students,
Wangfujing

Right: Chen Peng,
Architecture
Student,
Guangzhou Arts
Academy

Left: Michael Huang,
Designer,
Guangzhou Arts Academy

Right: Rock Chen,
Fashion Designer,
Guangzhou Arts Academy

Left: Creative manager,
Diandian, Beijing

Right: Shorts and hats
fan, Nanluoguxian

Left: Charlie Kan,
Fashion PR executive

Right: Japanese PR agent,
made-to-measure suit by
local tailor, Nanluoguxiang

Left: Xu Weijia,
Owner of 'Rich Gainer

Right: Patrick,
PR executive from
Hong Kong.

Above: Wang Xiaodong
(left) hair-dresser
Song Ying (right) works
in the media.

Right: Chris and
Hannah

Above: Aileen,
Software Designer

Right: Nicole,
Student

05.CASUALS

The success of the 2008 Beijing Olympics has fuelled an enthusiasm for all things sport-related in China. During the prosperity of the mid 'noughties' and the infiltration of Western ideas, the country's cultural outlook changed.

While ping-pong was traditionally heralded as the national game, the sports horizons of the younger generations have been broadened by digital media, online social networking and global sports brands media campaigns now aimed at Chinese people[20]. In turn, the government has begun to focus more on promoting football, tennis, basketball and other such sports that are traditionally dominated by the West. The National Basketball Association (NBA) are already making headway with the potential installation of 800,000 baskets in villages across the country, and twelve multi-purpose arenas in China's major cities[21].

The sport aesthetic has long been a popular one in China, but many more people are now eager to recreate, or be informed by, the appearance of their favourite athletes, while others have adopted a street look that alludes to an active lifestyle without being overtly sport-orientated.

Two distinct variations of the sportswear trend are manifested. 'Casual' types are mainstream consumers who wear toned-down sports apparel, giving the wearer the impression of being energetic and youthful without the labour of exercise itself. These individuals are often in their mid- to late twenties and do not necessarily have a sporting lifestyle or devote themselves to specific brands, but take pride in the quality of their appearance and prioritise comfort and presentation when it comes to selecting their clothes. The Casual tribe member tends to wear adaptable clothing that takes functionality and style into consideration, and will be likely to opt for the 'casual' ranges designed by sports brands. With a relatively slow fashion turnover of two seasons per year, many members of this tribe are less concerned with trends than durable quality, diversity of application, comfort and timeless presentation. The silhouettes of the clothes reflect the relaxed approach of this group, with loose-fitting T-shirts, cargo shorts and slouch bags being dominant features. Within this category is a further sub-tribe of the more fashion-focused, who will mix one or two sport-centric items to finish a fashion casual look – for example, gaudy-coloured Reebok trainers might accompany a pair of relaxed jeans, or a loud, oversized sports bag might set off an otherwise muted outfit. For this group there is slightly more emphasis on individuality, and logos are kept to a subtle and sophisticated minimum.

798 Art District, Beijing

The Sports Fan members of the tribe, conversely, engage regularly in sports and dress accordingly. The 19-year-old student Liu Shu represents a mass of like-minded peers when he claims that his life is occupied by basketball 80 per cent of the time, stating emphatically that he 'would give up sleep to play[22].' Younger, teenage students dominate this sub-tribe, in which sports apparel is transferred with effortless confidence from the courts and pitches, where they practice, to the bars, galleries and city streets of China. Foreign brands such as Nike, Kappa and Adidas are generally favoured by consumers, and in the same vein, the most idolised sports icons are not Chinese – international celebrities like Beckham, Jordan and Ronaldinho are held in the limelight. According to sweatshirt sales, Chinese basketball hero Yao Ming is not the biggest NBA star in China. Instead, the Chinese are purchasing jerseys adorned with the names of American NBA players Kobe Bryant and Kevin Garnett. Ming, though still recognised for his athletic capabilities, is just tenth on the list[23]. English football shirts are also out-selling all others in China, followed by Brazil, Argentina and Italy, and a substantial 78 per cent of Chinese sports fans are interested in international football while only 31 per cent prefer local football teams[24]. Perhaps the allure of success represented by these international sports heroes is the reason for this foreign idolisation. Sports Fans will literally display their passion for sports about their person; whether a team player or a spectator, a key garment is the jersey of a favourite player or athlete, and the proud, diehard wearer will combine this with matching shorts to complete the kit. 'Sneaker culture' is particularly prominent, with many young people valuing the brand of their trainers over their clothes. Although Chinese brand Li Ning is worn, Sports Fans will more often than not be found in a pair of Nikes – particularly the basketball enthusiasts. Impractical accessories such as jewellery are usually minimal and not too important in either subcategories of this group, but bold sweatbands or rubber bracelets are sometimes used to complete an outfit's sporty aesthetic.

Sporting activities are a fundamental part of the Chinese education system and are generally valued as a healthy and fun aspect of daily life – it is estimated that 300 million Chinese are taking part in regular sports activities. 'By 2010, the Nationwide Physical Fitness Program aims to have 40 per cent of China's population participating in routine physical exercise[25].' With such a high importance placed on the nation's physical fitness, it is unsurprising that the Casuals sports tribe has such a vast following.

Liu Shiping,
Likes her clothes to
have 'attitude'.

Deng Jianbo,
Interior Designer
798 District,
Beijing

Below and left: Jax Lin,
Fashion Designer;
798 District, Beijing

Opposite: Lomo,
Shop Owner / Designer,
Diwang Square

Wayne Lin,
Reporter

Rita Lo,
Works for a Hong Kong
based streetwear
magazine

Above and right: Lin Lin,
Stylist, Olympic Village
Beijing

Opposite: Zhu Jiajie

老弱病残伤专
用车停靠点
The Elder、 the Little
the Disabled and the Injured Parking

Opposite: Student, Gulou

Below and left: Crowds at Dongsi club, Beijing

Heng, Student
Yue Fu, Beijing

Students outside Raffles
Design Institute

Right: Leila, Fashion student
Raffles Design Institute
Design Institute

Below: Kini Lee, Photographer
University Town Beijing

Sports fans during 2008
Olympics, Beijing

Students outside
Dongdan
Basketball Stadium

Li Chi, manager of
Mao Live House,
Beijing, and founder of
Beardy Live Music

Crowd in Wangfujing,
Beijing

Left: Jianwei Wang,
Music Student,
University Town

Above: Amateur Tennis
Player, SoHo

Right and below: Sports fan
attending Volleyball game
at Good Luck, Beijing
during the 2008 Olympics in
Chao Yang Park.

Right and left: Sport Casual at Nike basketball event, Beijing

Opposite: Zhu Ning, Student

Top: Student
(plays for his school basketball team)

Above: Sports fan
(plays for local team on weekends)

Right: Nike basketball enthusiast,
Beijing

Opposite: Chelsea FC John Terry
fan

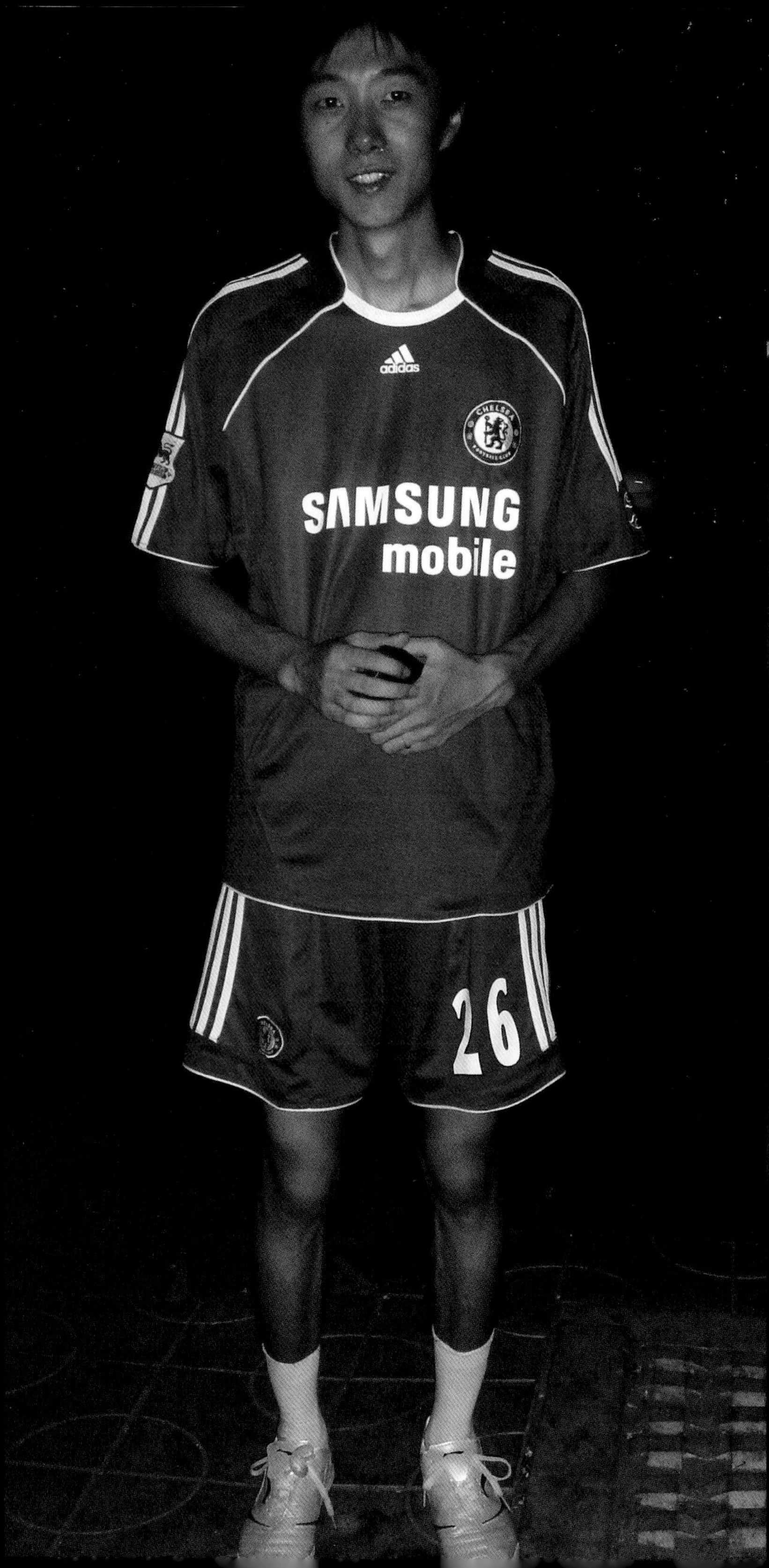
adidas
SAMSUNG
mobile
26

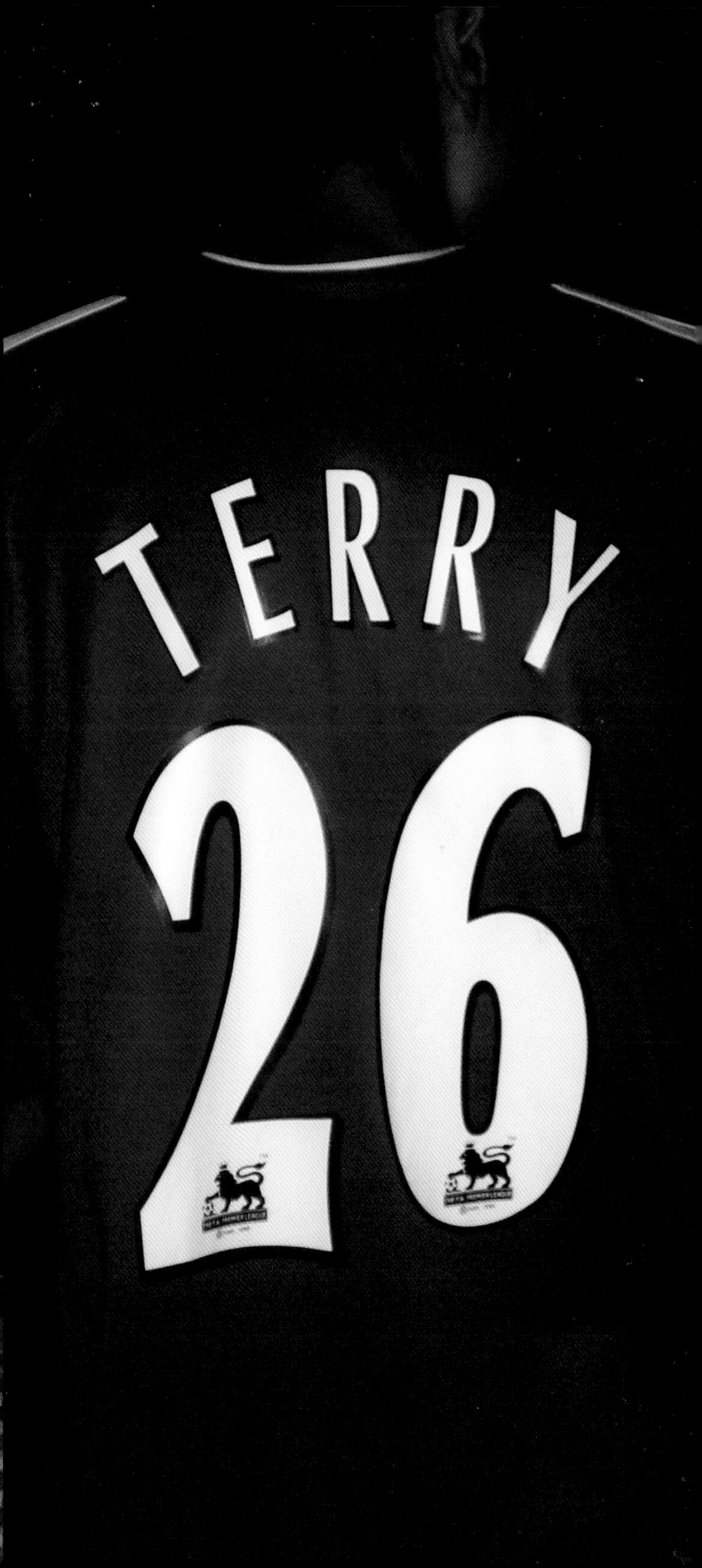
TERRY
26

Above and left: Portugal football fan

Opposite left: Holland fan at ease in 798 gallery bookstore

Opposite right: AC Milan Kaka fan, Beijing

FOOTNOTES

Alternatives | pp10–11

1 http://www.charlesfrith.com/2008/04/beijing-fashion-and-trends.html

2 http://www.smartshanghai.com/blog/97/Rebel_Ink_Shanghai_Style_shanghai

3 http://www.coolhunting.com/archives/2007/03/chinese_indepen.php

4 http://www.coolhunting.com/archives/2007/03/chinese_indepen.php

Iconics | pp40–41

5 http://online.wsj.com/public/article_print/SB121752752638401551.html

6 www.buybuybeijing.com

Hip Hop | pp68–69

7 May 31, 2007 China Youth Culture Study Provides New Insight + Trend Forecasting in Fashion, Technology, Communication, Entertainment, Sports, Music

8 Xi Guatou, Vox Pop Interview

9 Vox Pop Interview

10 http://www.chinadaily.com.cn/cndy/2007-11/10/content_6244708.htm

11 http://www.chinadaily.com.cn/cndy/2007-11/10/content_6244708.htm

12 Vox Pop Interview

Fashionistas | pp94–95

13 Vox Pop interview

14 http://www.cibmagazine.com.cn/Features/Focus.asp?id=396&battle_of_the_brands.html

15 Personal taste and family face: Luxury consumption in Confucian and western societies - Nancy Y. Wong 1, Aaron C. Ahuvia 2

16 http://www.viiphoto.com/detailStory.php?news_id=174

17 April 13, 2008 *Sunday Times*

18 http://news.cnet.com/8301-13641_3-9912252-44.html

19 http://chinayouthology.com/blog/

Casual Sports | pp126–127

20 http://www.washingtonpost.com/wp-dyn/content/story/2008/08/13/ST2008081303823.html

21 http://sports.espn.go.com/oly/summer08/basketball/news/story?id=3542013

22 Nikevp3

23 http://www.streetball.com/profiles/blog/show?id=1024073%3ABlogPost%3A324028"

24 http://www.footballshirtculture.com/20070628416/fans/england-football-shirts-no-1-in-china.html

25 http://english.gov.cn/2006-02/08/content_182552.htm

CONTRIBUTORS

ZHENG ZHENG
A product designer who graduated from Central Saint Martins College of Art & Design, London, in 2005, Zheng is now based in South China, specializing in bathroom product and furniture design, and also works as a columnist writer for national magazines.

JELLYMON
Jellymon / JMGS is a multi-discipline design studio that creates and provides design, fashion, artwork, toys, lifestyle products, photography, branding and creative / art direction. Jellymon was founded by Lin Lin and Sam Jacobs, who met at Chelsea School of Art in 2002 and have been working together ever since.

MR.223
Lin Zhipeng resides in Beijing. He is a photographer, fashion creative, magazine editor, and founder of the independent photography fashion magazine "TOO".
blog: http://finger_blue.blogcn.com

ALICIA LEE
Fashion designer, living in Beijing. After graduating in International Trade, she studied and worked in the Fashion Design Department at Beijing Raffles Design Institute. She recently started her own store called NOISE and launched her own brand WillowWillow, a small ready-to-wear label, as well as providing couture service for young professionals.

ALEXANDER DLUZAK
Residing in Berlin, Alexander is currently working as a journalist, film-maker and photographer.

SOMETHINK STUDIO
Based in Guangzhou, China, it is an organisation dedicated to commercial and modern art exchanges. It was founded by PACO HRD, a young successful advertiser, and ALEX SO, a fashion photographer and founder of COLDTEA magazine.

SomeThink Studio.

NELS FRYE

From Massachusetts, Nels M. N. Frye has lived in Taipei, Hong Kong, Hangzhou, Chengdu and Beijing. Working as a business consultant, freelance writer, photographer, stylist, and English teacher, Nels is also Creative Director for Senli and Frye, a rapidly expanding custom menswear boutique in Beijing.

PESTAÑA RUI

A Portuguese photojournalist who lived in China during 2008. During that year he graduated with a Masters degree in International Photojournalism taught by the University of Bolton and Dalian Image Art College in China. Some of his most notable 'Chinese' works include the coverage of the Sichuan earthquake and the issue of sustainable ecological business.

PAULINE REN

A fashion merchandiser who graduated from Northumbria University in Fashion Marketing and Management in 2006, she now works in a fashion studio, specialising in window displays, consultation and styling, as well as graphic design.

ADDITIONAL CONTRIBUTORS:

Cookie, Jason, Sahra Malik, David Zellaby, Paolo di Montegnacco, and David Gedawei

SAINTS NEW BLOOD: RAW TREND

Helps decode and decipher emerging art, design and socio-cultural trends that are still being shaped at Central Saint Martins, which holds what we believe to be the most creative, international and influential group of 20-something early adopters. We couple this insight with an international network of contributors for a truly global perspective.

Editor: Kevin Tallon

Written Research: Amy Knight, Mari Santos

Visual Research: Neus Rodriguez, Philip Gamble

ACKNOWLEDGEMENTS

For all their help, support and efforts, I would like to thank: Neus Rodriguez, Amy Knight, Mari Santos, Dani Salvadori, Yann Mathias, Angy Wang, Nels Frye, Alicia Li Kun, Tim Hoar, Sam Jacobs, Pauline Ren, Zheng Zheng, Sahra Malik, Lin Zhipeng, DongXiang Sports and all ther others that I may have forgotten.

The photographers listed below are responsible for the images in this book:

Alicia Li Kun: pages 18, 19, 20, 21, 22 (right), 24, 25, 26 27, 31 (top right), 32, 33, 34, 44 (left), 45, 51, 54, 55, 58, 59, 62, 63 (left), 64 (right), 74, 75, 76, 80, 81, 82, 83, 84 (right), 86, 87, 93 (left), 94, 98, 99, 101, 103, 104, 106, 107, 108, 114 (right), 115, 116, 118, 130, 131, 132, 134, 135, 138, 139 (left), 141, 142 (right), 143 (right), 144, 145, 146, 150, 152 (right), 153, 154, 155 (right)

Alexander Dluzak: pages 71 (left column lower), 88 (top), 89,

Cookie Zuo: pages 18 (top right), 28 (left and right columns), 35 (left column), 111 (left column), 113 (right), 147 (middle), 152 (left Column)

Cythia: pages 100 (Left), 102

Jason Meng: pages 23, 28 (centre), 35 (right), 71 (left column middle), 88 (lower), 109 (left), 114 (left column), 117,

Jellymon: pages 42, 63 (right column), 136,

Liu Misi: pages 60, 91, 93 (right), 95, 96 (left), 97, 112, 147 (left)

Lin Zhipeng [Mr. 223]: pages 36, 37, 38, 39, 41, 67 (right), 127

Nels Frye: pages 12, 13, 14 (left), 15, 16, 17, 50, 52, 53, 56, 57, 61, 64 (left), 78 (left), 79 (top right), 105, 109 (right), 122, 123, 124, 125, 143 (left),

Paco HRD: pages 29, 43, 44 (right), 46, 47, 48, 78 (right), 79 (left), 84 (left), 119 (right), 120, 142 (left),

Pauline Ren: pages 43 (middle and right), 73, 77, 79 (lower right), 85, 96 (right), 113 (middle and left), 129, 137, 147 (right column), 149, 151

Rui Pestana: pages 69, 70, 71 (top and right), 92 **Paco:** 43, 46, 47, 48, 66, 101

Sahra Malik: pages 22, 26 (right), 30, 31 (left), 72, 100 (right), 139 (right), 148, 155 (left)

Ye Jian Guang: pages 11, 14 (right)

Zheng Zheng: pages 66, 67 (left), 110, 111 (right), 121 (left), 133, 140